31 Days
of Prayer
for
My Child

Books by the Yates family:

And Then I Had Kids: Encouragement for Mothers of Young Children, Susan Alexander Yates

And Then I Had Teenagers: Encouragement for Parents of Teens and Preteens, Susan Alexander Yates

Character Matters! Raising Kids with Values That Last, John and Susan Yates

How a Man Prays for His Family, John W. Yates

The Incredible Four-Year Adventure: Finding Real Faith, Fun, and Friendship at College, John Yates III and Chris Yates

Building a Home Full of Grace, John and Susan Yates and Family

31 Days of Prayer for My Teen, Susan Alexander Yates

31 Days of Prayer for My Child

A Parent's Guide

SUSAN ALEXANDER YATES

ALLISON YATES GASKINS

BakerBooks

Grand Rapids, Michigan

© 2004 by Susan Alexander Yates and Allison Yates Gaskins

Published by Baker Books
a division of Baker Publishing Group
P.O. Box 6287, Grand Rapids, MI 49516-6287
www.bakerbooks.com

Printed in the United States of America

Library of Congress Cataloging-in-Publication Data
Yates, Susan Alexander.
    31 days of prayer for my child : a parent's guide / Susan Alexander
Yates, Allison Yates Gaskins.
        p.   cm.
    ISBN 0-8010-1273-2 (pbk.)
    1. Parents—Prayer-books and devotions—English. I. Title: Thirty-one
days of prayer for my child. II. Gaskins, Allison Yates. III. Title.
BV4529.Y375 2005
242′.845—dc22   2004020042

Scripture is taken from the HOLY BIBLE, NEW INTERNATIONAL VERSION®. NIV®. Copyright © 1973, 1978, 1984 by International Bible Society. Used by permission of Zondervan. All rights reserved.

To our
Thursday morning girlfriends in McLean, Virginia
and our
Wednesday morning girlfriends in Ligonier, Pennsylvania:
Your friendship and partnership have brought
immeasurable joy to our journeys.
Your lives speak Proverbs 25:11 to us.
Thank you.

Contents

Acknowledgments

To Callie, Will Jr., Tucker, Sylvia, Tobin, and all who follow in this newest generation—we promise to keep praying! We love you!

To our husbands, John and Will; thanks for being the number one men in our lives!

To Vicki Crumpton, many thanks for your partnership and excellent editing. And thanks to all of the team at Baker Books. You *all* do great work!

How to Use This Book

As parents of young children we *know* we *need* to pray, but we are often so overwhelmed with our children's needs (and our own) that we don't know where or how to begin.

This book will help you!

We have structured these prayers in a format that loosely follows David's prayers in the Psalms. They begin with a statement telling God "this is how I'm feeling" about my child and where I am in mothering. Then they continue by affirming who we know God to be and by bringing a specific need to God in prayer. You may notice as you read these prayers that the opening paragraph expresses a personal sentiment that you may not always feel. That is okay! Feel free to express your own sentiments to God. As you move into the main body of the prayer you will find that it is designed to help you pray in harmony with various promises that God has given us in Scripture. If the prayer for the day doesn't seem to "fit" your situation, you might want to skip to another day using a prayer that expresses your current concern.

Our goal in this project is not for you to merely repeat formatted prayers but to begin the habit of speaking to God about your specific needs on a daily basis. Intercession (praying for others) is a very personal journey! In addition, you will find that although most of these prayers are for your child, some pertain more directly to you, the mother. We absolutely *must* pray for ourselves. Even Jesus did!

There are two simple ways to use this book.

You can use it as a daily prayer for your child and yourself by matching each prayer to the day's date (pray Day 1 on the first of the month, etc.). With this method you'll be able to cultivate the habit of regular daily prayer for your child and in the process experience the joy of a regular time to let God himself encourage *you*. By praying in this way, you will receive the benefit of exploring issues that might not have occurred to you.

Second, you'll note that each prayer has a particular topic, so if you prefer, you can go directly to the topic best expressing your concern and pray that specific prayer. Prayers are listed by topic in the table of contents.

The inspiration for this book comes from Susan's book *And Then I Had Kids: Encouragement for Mothers of Young Children*. That book deals with the challenges we face as we raise our young children. In it you will find practical guidance in handling many of the issues you will be praying about in this book. The intent is for this book of prayers to be a companion to the larger book. Additional help is also available in John and Susan's book *Character Matters! Raising Kids with Values That Last*.

Further information about these two books and other helpful resources can be found in appendix 3.

In the prayers we have tried to balance using "he" or "she" ("son" or "daughter"). We felt that using "he/she" would detract so we have chosen one or the other to use in each prayer. Please adjust the gender to suit your needs.

After each day's prayer you will find a series of activities that can personalize and deepen your prayer time. Let the printed prayer be a basis for creating your own prayer for your child and write it out in the space provided. When you use the book next month, you'll be encouraged to see how God has answered your prayer. List one character trait of God that has been brought to your mind by the prayer or the verses. (For example, *Thank you, God, that you are always faithful.*) Throughout the day, take time to think about what his *faithfulness* means to you. Finally, write out one promise of Scripture from the verses listed (after the prayer) that seems to speak to you at this time. You may want to look up these references in your Bible or use a concordance to discover similar verses. God will encourage you with his Word!

Perhaps praying for your child is a new experience; you may be thinking, *I'm not even sure I ought to be talking to God. I don't feel that I know him in the same way others do.* If this is a question in your heart, we invite you to turn to appendix 1 in the back of the book for some personal encouragement *before* you begin to pray for your child.

However you choose to use this book, we pray that you will find yourself not simply going to God with the latest issue about your child but also falling in love with a God who cares about every detail in your child's life *and* in yours.

Introduction

'm not a very good pray-er.

I'd like to be.

I have visions of locking myself away in my room for an hour every day, fervently praying with my eyes closed and a "direct line" open to God. I even have a Bible, a prayer journal, and a comfy chair to sit in!

But there's a pile of laundry in that chair. Pages have been torn out of my Bible, and my son has scribbled on nearly every page of my prayer notebook. In fact, he carries it around the house and thinks it's his. The lock on my bedroom door is broken, and I'm afraid it's probably illegal to lock my children away from me anyway (though sometimes I'd really like to!).

Do *you* ever feel like this? If you do, you must be the mother of young children too.

The responsibility of raising my small children weighs on me like a brick. I am terrified of failure. I want to pray for my children—I really, really do. I have learned that even if I do things "the right way," the way my mother, Dr. Dobson, and all the experts tell me to (that is, if I had time to listen to their broadcasts and read all their books), and even if I follow all the rules of "good parenting" things will not automatically turn out "just fine."

Parenting is not a fair and equal equation. A + B does *not* always = C. Just when my infant starts sleeping through the night, the toddler begins wetting the bed. Once that is settled, my kindergartener starts having nightmares. Tomorrow I'll wake up and they'll be teenagers, and then I won't sleep because they'll be dating or driving. And then next week they'll be grown-ups, grateful to me but wanting to do their "own thing." Right now I'm changing their diapers and making lunches and drowning in laundry, and these are the most formative days of my children's lives!

I am so afraid of failing at this job. I dove into motherhood thinking I would be okay if I just did what my mother did (she's a great lady and I turned out fine, didn't I?), but now I realize that isn't as simple as it sounds.

HELP!

I don't know how to survive at this mothering thing. I don't know what to pray. I don't know how to be a "good mom." I don't know how to make my children turn out well and love God and glorify him with their lives. My mother keeps telling me she felt the very same way. Hopefully one day I'll start to believe her! We both agree on one thing, however: No one knows innately how to be a good mom. Every one of us is inadequate. That's why each of us, in fact every mother who ever *lived*, desperately needs God. He *is* adequate!

I do know a few things for sure:

God created me and loves me.

God created my children and brought them into our family for a specific reason. He cares about their well-being even more than I do. (Is that possible?)

He listens when I pray.

And, perhaps the greatest relief of all, when I am weak (especially as a mother!) he is strong.

14

I long selfishly to be known as "a woman of prayer"—because I am not one—yet. I do not pray often enough, long enough, thoroughly enough—even for my children. Often I just breathe out a "God bless them and keep them safe through the night" as I sink into the pillow. Often I growl in frustration, "God, I cannot handle this. You're gonna have to step in here, please."

And he does!

And he will!

One thing I have learned as the grown daughter of an ever-praying mother: *God is faithful, and he will answer our prayers.* Who I am, who my mother is, who my children are—these things are not nearly as important as who God is, and the fact that he is our source for everything in life and mothering. Raising these precious children may be my job right now, but really, it's all up to him. We can and we *must* come to him in prayer about every aspect of their lives. We will mother these babies, but God in his infinite wisdom and mercy will raise them up to be his own.

When Jesus's mother met her cousin Elizabeth during their pregnancies, Elizabeth spoke a precious blessing upon Mary. She said: "Blessed is she who has believed that what the Lord has said to her will be accomplished!" (Luke 1:45).

You and I can claim this blessing too. Believe that God hears your prayers for your children and that he who began a good work in them—and you—will accomplish it.

Let's pray, together, for our children.

ALLISON

And I will do whatever you ask in my name, so that the Son may bring glory to the Father. You may ask me for anything in my name, and I will do it.

JOHN 14:13–14

If There's a "Perfect Parent," It's Not Me!

Too often we see ourselves as failures. We have in mind an image of what the "Perfect Parent" looks like, and in raising a particular child we realize how far short we fall. What does God expect of me and why did he choose to give me *this* child?

God, I do not know how to handle this child. She knows just how to push all those buttons that get me fired up and angry—and she's still so little! Sometimes she reflects the worst of me and I feel frozen. Couldn't you have given me an easier child until I knew more about this parenting thing? I feel as if I am really messing up with this one. It's overwhelming to think that you have entrusted this particular child to me.

My girlfriend is no help. *She* seems to have it all together. *She* doesn't lose her temper. *She* studies her Bible and prays. *She* even *looks* nice. She makes parenting look easy. Is she for real? What's her secret, Lord, and when are you going to fill me in?

Father, I'm so glad that you don't really expect me to be a perfect parent.* There aren't any! Not among my friends, not even in the Bible. We all mess up, but *you* don't.

You did *not* make a mistake in giving me this child.* You created her with our family in mind. I know you are choosing each of my children specifically, sending them to us in the exact birth order you desire and giving each one a distinct personality. I know you are giving them to us not merely to raise but also in order for you to use each one to grow *me* into the person you have created *me* to be.*

Make me open to what you might be teaching me through this child. Remind me that in my imperfection you are perfect, and in my weakness you are strong.* Teach me something special through this child. Use her to reveal to me fresh insights about your character.

For the LORD *is good and his love endures forever; his faithfulness continues through all generations.*

PSALM 100:5

Scripture references (in order of starred references in prayer): Psalm 103:13–14; James 1:7; Psalm 102:28; 2 Corinthians 12:9

My prayer for my child today:

The character trait of God that I will focus on today: (Thank you, Lord, that you are . . .)

A promise of Scripture for today:

18

Keep This Child Safe

Most mothers will tell you that their greatest fears are for their child's safety. We would gladly give our own lives to protect our children. It is normal to worry about their safety—one glance at the nightly news reinforces all our worst fears. Yet, we do not need to live lives imprisoned by this fear.

Lord, I know it's unreasonable, but I have this fear that the moment I turn my back or leave my child with a baby-sitter, something terrible is going to happen! Sometimes my fear for his physical safety is so real that it takes my breath away. I know I can really do nothing to control all the circumstances of his life, but I still try! Isn't that part of a mother's job description?

Today, Father, I ask you one simple thing. Please keep my child safe!

You know what this child means to me. You care about both of us even more than I can comprehend. From the lips of children and infants you have ordained praise!* You have said that the greatest in your kingdom must be like a little child.* You asked little children to come to you and be near you, and you blessed them.* You call each of us the apple of your eye* so I know you care about my child!

You shield the ones you love like an eagle that stirs up its nest and hovers over its young.* You even fiercely defended children, saying that if anyone brought them harm it would be better to have a stone tied around his neck and be thrown into the sea.* So, Lord, I know that my child's safety is something that concerns you greatly. Thank you. I do trust your will, Father—but I know it is a reality of life that some harm may come to my child. Sometimes I fear that you may allow pain to be part of your plan for him, and I admit that scares me.

You have told us not to worry, Lord—that it won't even add a single hour to our lives.* That is far easier said than done, but I will try! I give you my fears today, Lord. I know that you are God and I am not. I know that your angels surround my child and that these angels see your face in heaven.* Thank you, Father.

He who dwells in the shelter of the Most High will rest in the shadow of the Almighty. I will say of the LORD, "He is my refuge and my fortress, my God, in whom I trust."

PSALM 91:1–2

Scripture references (in order of starred references in prayer): Psalm 8:2; Matthew 18:4; Mark 10:14–16;

Psalm 17:8; Deuteronomy 32:11; Matthew 18:6; Matthew 6:27, 31; Matthew 18:10

My prayer for my child today:

The character trait of God that I will focus on today: (Thank you, Lord, that you are . . .)

A promise of Scripture for today:

Today I Accomplished Nothing

Mothers with small children oftentimes feel that they don't accomplish very much. Their days seem to blur with repetition of the same tasks and no real feeling of progress. This can even be downright depressing! "Does anyone else feel like I do? Does anyone understand?"

Lord, today I am frustrated!

I feel as if I have accomplished nothing. My house and my life are in worse shape now than they were when I woke up this morning—and it didn't help when my husband came home this evening and asked innocently, "Hi, honey, what did you get done today?" I didn't get anything done. I just got through it.

God, you remember when I had a job outside the home

and I felt appreciated. I set goals and accomplished them. I felt a sense of progress. I had job reviews and incentives and a salary! But *today* I haven't made much progress. The house I cleaned this morning is dirtier than ever. The kids haven't started quoting Bible verses or even picked up the toys I asked them to. No one has appreciated me. What child would say, "Hey, Mom, you're doing a great job of raising me!"?

I'm feeling lower than low, and I really need a little encouragement that this is all worthwhile.

Thank you, Jesus, that you understand how I feel.* When your neighbors in Nazareth rejected you and tried to throw you over a cliff, you must have been discouraged and wondered if you were accomplishing anything worthwhile.* You must have been frustrated in the Garden of Gethsemane when you asked three of your disciples to watch and pray with you and they fell asleep instead.*

Father, when my child faces frustration and discouragement in life, remind him that your love for him is never wavering. It is always the same,* always higher than the heavens.*

I am so grateful that you understand how I feel *and* that your love for me is not based on my accomplishments. You don't love me because I'm a good wife or a good mother or because I'm successful. Instead you love me simply because I belong to you.

The LORD your God is with you, he is mighty to save. He will take great delight in you, he will quiet you with his love, he will rejoice over you with singing.
                                        ZEPHANIAH 3:17

Scripture references (in order of starred references in prayer): Hebrews 2:17–18; Luke 4:28–30; Matthew 26:36–41; Hebrews 13:8; Psalm 108:4

23

My prayer for my child today:

The character trait of God that I will focus on today:
(Thank you, Lord, that you are . . .)

A promise of Scripture for today:

Taking Time to Wonder

When you're a mother it's so easy to rush through your days, meeting one need after another. It's easy to focus on the things that need to be done now and on the voices clamoring for your attention. It is hard to slow down and observe. Do our children have something deeper to teach us about wonder?

Father, as I hold my tiny baby and look at her varied expressions, I'm overwhelmed. It's so amazing to see her growing. I feel as if she's changing right before my eyes! Today I watched her respond to light and movement. Her little eyes got huge as she watched the ceiling fan going around and around. She seems to notice the simplest details that are in front of her—faces, shadows and light, movement. She doesn't miss a thing. Her expression is one of wonder.

As I watch her I realize that I have lost my own capacity for awe and wonder. I am missing so much. I'm too busy

25

just trying to get through the day, rushing to finish one more thing, trying to keep some sort of order in the house. Taking time to marvel at your creation seems like a lost luxury. But it isn't. You want me to take time to notice the little things around me—funny expressions on my child's face, a delicate flower, a deep-red sunset, even the light beams that dance around my house! Your greatness is on display in every direction if only my eyes and my heart can be open to see.* When I delight in the works of your hands I bring you joy!

O Father, slow me down. Help me to take in your beauty of creation. There is no one like you. You are majestic in holiness, awesome in glory, always working wonders.* Take me to a deeper appreciation of all your mighty works.* Sharpen my observation skills so that I don't miss one detail of my child's growth. I long to notice each distinct expression, each awakening in her eyes as she observes something new. Use her to awaken in me a fresh sense of awe and wonder at what you have done.

As she grows up in a world that is becoming more and more "man made," protect her from losing her childlike sense of awe. Give her eyes that will always marvel at *your* creation and *your* works. Keep her from taking them for granted. Help us both to become people who live in awe of your majesty.*

I will meditate on all your works and consider all your mighty deeds. Your ways, O God, are holy. What god is so great as our God?

PSALM 77:12–13

Scripture references (in order of starred references in prayer): Psalm 92:5; Exodus 15:11; 1 Chronicles 16:27–36; Psalm 93:1

My prayer for my child today:

The character trait of God that I will focus on today:
(Thank you, Lord, that you are . . .)

A promise of Scripture for today:

Sibling Rivalry

We want our homes to be places of love and laughter. But so often we feel as if the walls are falling down around us as the screaming and yelling reach a crescendo. We want to teach our children to love one another with words and actions. It's so hard when the house seems more like a battleground!

Lord, you know that I long for my children to love one another. I want them to be each other's "best friend." I want them to stand up for each other and to defend one another against the world. I want them to have *fun* together and to enjoy the company of our family. But often it seems my children fight over everything, no matter how small! I know that it takes many years for children to grow up into friends. Help me to remember this when I expect instant results.

Sometimes I am so frustrated as their mean words fly in pointless arguments. Lord Jesus, you had siblings.* You had earthly parents too.* Pour out on me your wisdom to combat this monster of sibling rivalry. Your Word reminds me how good and pleasant it is when brothers and sisters dwell together in unity. Bestow this blessing upon my children, Father.* Let them find great joy in our family relationships, so that one day we all might glorify your name together.*

I don't know the wisest way to handle this. You understand—your disciples fought over silly things such as which one of them was the greatest!* Show me when to step in to settle my children's arguments and when to let them work out their problems themselves. But Lord, help them learn to settle their disagreements without hurting one another!

You are the God of love and unity. You desire even more than I do that our home be characterized by love rather than harsh words—you commanded this.* Soften the hearts of our family members. Clothe each of us with compassion, kindness, humility, gentleness, and patience. Teach us to bear with one another's faults and to forgive one another in the same way that you forgive us. Bind us together in the perfect unity of your love and let peace rule in our home!*

---

*Then the LORD came down in the cloud . . .
and proclaimed his name. . . . The LORD, the
compassionate and gracious God, slow to anger,
abounding in love and faithfulness, maintaining
love to thousands, and forgiving wickedness.*

EXODUS 34:5–7

*Scripture references (in order of starred references in prayer):
Mark 3:31; Matthew 1:16; Psalm 133:1, 3; Romans 15:6;
Mark 9:33–34; John 15:17; Colossians 3:12–15*

My prayer for my child today:

The character trait of God that I will focus on today:
(Thank you, Lord, that you are . . .)

A promise of Scripture for today:

A Hunger
for God's Word

Our culture says there is no absolute truth. Every-thing is relative, and whoever argues best wins the case. Yet, we know that there is a truth, and it is found in God's Word. I long for my child to develop a love for that truth.

Father, where has truth gone? I look around and see confusion. I fear for my child. Many attractive people will speak falsehoods to her. How will she know who is right? Others will try to lead her astray. How will she make wise decisions? She will long for security. Where will she find it? While she's young she'll listen to me, but there will come a

31

time when she may not want to—and I'm not always right anyway. *I* don't know all truth. Her security can't be based on me. I'll let her down.

Father, you *alone* are the way, the truth, and the life.* You have given us the Scriptures as the proclamation of your truths. Your Word is all true, and it is your love letter to me and to my child.

Your Word isn't simply another collection of wise sayings. Instead, it is living power! Your Word is described as sharper than a double-edged sword, able to penetrate my soul and spirit and to judge my thoughts and attitudes.* Your Word is the only thing that lasts forever!*

Your disciple Peter said that we are to long for the pure milk of your Word just as my child longs to nurse at my breast.* My breast milk is created to supply everything my infant needs. It lacks nothing. What a beautiful picture of how your Word contains everything I need and everything my child will need to live in your world.*

Father, as my child grows up she will hunger for things that only you can supply. She may not recognize her hunger or know where to go to be fed. I ask you to give her a hunger for your Word. Give her the desire to spend time reading your Scriptures. Give her models who uphold the authority of your Word and who spend time studying it. There are so many things I want for my child, but more than anything I pray that she will fall in love with your Word. Only in this will she find true fulfillment.*

Your word is a lamp to my feet and a light for my path.

PSALM 119:105

Scripture references (in order of starred references in prayer): John 14:6; Hebrews 4:12; Matthew 24:35; 1 Peter 2:2; 2 Samuel 22:31; John 4:13–14

My prayer for my child today:

The character trait of God that I will focus on today:
(Thank you, Lord, that you are . . .)

A promise of Scripture for today:

My Child's Future Spouse

Most of us hope that one day our child will fall in love. At this stage of parenting it's hard to imagine, but it's true. Before we know it, a special young man or young woman will enter our child's life. It's not too early to pray for this person!

Today, Father, I'm thinking about marriage. Not mine, but my son's.

It seems a long way off, but it is so important that I know I need to begin praying now. Somewhere I hope there is a little girl who will one day be my daughter-in-law.

Our culture keeps redefining what constitutes marriage. Purity is scorned. Temptation is everywhere. "My rights" are considered more important than another's needs. There are fewer families with both a mom and a dad. Not many are committed until *death do us part* but instead *until one of us becomes unhappy.*

Father, I know that you call some to singleness and many to marry.* Neither is a "higher" calling than the other. Yet God, you know that my heart's desire is for a spouse for my child. And you have said that I can pray about absolutely anything.* I ask that you would be preparing a special little girl for him to marry. Give her a tender heart. Help her to come to know you at a young age. Surround her with love. Teach her to share. Protect her from temptation and danger. Keep her pure in her heart and in her relationships. Help her to grow to love you with all her heart. Surround her with godly women who will disciple her.* Bring her into my son's life in your perfect time. Please be preparing me to love this young woman as if she were my own daughter.

I also pray for her parents. (And Lord, I hope there are parents somewhere praying for me as I raise my son!) Give them wisdom as they raise her.* Guide them as they teach her self-discipline. Encourage them when they feel like failures.* Show them how to encourage her faith. Help them to grow in their knowledge of you. If they are discouraged today, lift their spirits.

Thank you, Father, for caring about my child's future.* Thank you that you hear my prayers and will answer. Thank you that you are already at work in my child's life and in the life of his future spouse.*

Now to him who is able to do immeasurably more than all we ask or imagine, according to his power that is at work within us, to him be glory in the church and in Christ Jesus throughout all generations, for ever and ever! Amen.

EPHESIANS 3:20–21

35

Scripture references (in order of starred references in prayer):
1 Corinthians 7:1–2; Philippians 4:6–7; Titus 2:4; James
1:5; Romans 8:1; Jeremiah 29:11; Philippians 2:13

My prayer for my child today:

The character trait of God that I will focus on today:
(Thank you, Lord, that you are . . .)

A promise of Scripture for today:

Working Outside the Home

Mothers who work outside the home face a constant battle. How do they operate fully in two worlds and feel as if they are succeeding? They often feel torn between their loved ones and their career and misunderstood by their peers. If you do not work outside the home, use this day to pray for your friends who do.

Lord, some days I feel as if I have the best of both worlds; other days I feel as if I have the worst. You have given me a precious family to nurture, and you have given me a professional life to help provide for this family. I love both of these "lives" (on most days, anyway), and I want to honor you in both endeavors. Trying to do this is difficult, though, and I often feel as if I'm barely keeping my head above water!

Sometimes I feel misunderstood by my professional peers *as well as* my stay-at-home friends. It is nearly impossible to feel successful at work and at home at the same time. Sometimes I feel like I'm failing at both! And the worst thing about it is that the other women who are in my same situation are all as busy as I am—so there's not much free time to be with each other for encouragement!

Father, I need your perspective. It is so easy to focus on the demands I feel instead of the blessings you have given me—so easy to fall into the trap of complaining. I ask instead that you would give me a grateful heart.* Show me one specific thing to praise you for today.

Lord, you know my thoughts.* You know how I struggle.* You were constantly surrounded by people who wanted you to perform just one more miracle. It seemed no matter what you did, it wasn't enough for them!* You gave me talents that I use in my professional life and you also gave me a mother's heart. You know what is realistic and necessary for this season in my life and what is not.* Please show me when I have to lower my expectations. Give me clarity on things that I need to let go of or postpone and confirm the things I need to do. Help me to prioritize* and to be thankful.

The Lord *will fulfill his purpose for me; your love, O* Lord, *endures forever—do not abandon the works of your hands.*

Psalm 138:8

Scripture references (in order of starred references in prayer): Psalm 21:6; Psalm 139:1–4; Psalm 147:5; Luke 8:40–56; Ecclesiastes 3:1; Matthew 6:33

My prayer for my child today:

The character trait of God that I will focus on today:
(Thank you, Lord, that you are . . .)

A promise of Scripture for today:

Integrity

Raising kids with character in today's world is a challenge. Values are so confused that it's hard to know *where* to begin much less *how* to do it. How do we lay the groundwork for raising kids with values that will last?

Father, our world's standard seems to be, *"It doesn't matter what you do as long as no one gets hurt and no one finds out."* But God, your standard is to *"do what's right when no one is looking and no one will find out."* Your standard gets buried in the pressures of today. My child's instinct is to lie to keep from getting in trouble. It seems to come so naturally to her! Sometimes I don't think she consciously decides to tell a lie—it just spills right out of her mouth, because it's easier than the truth.

Sometimes it's easy to overlook her dishonesty. It was

only a "little thing." She might not have meant to lie. Disciplining her causes such a scene. But deception in "little things" will lead to dishonesty in big things. Your Word warns us of what we are seeing in our culture: dishonesty ultimately leads to downfall.*

Father, you detest lying lips but delight in those who are truthful.* You have called us to be people of complete integrity. Show me how to explain to my child what it means to be a truthful person. And God, you know it's not just my child. It's me too. I don't always tell the complete truth. Too often I think the end will justify the means. And I know that's wrong.

Forgive me, Lord. Make me like Job, who, in the midst of horrible circumstances, loss, and temptation, determined to maintain his integrity until death.*

Thank you for promising to teach my child (and me) and to guide us into all truth.* Continue to remind me to buckle the belt of truth around my waist!* Thank you that as we grow in integrity we will find security and will discover that truth brings freedom.*

If you hold to my teaching, you are really my disciples. Then you will know the truth, and the truth will set you free.

JOHN 8:31–32

Scripture references (in order of starred references in prayer): Proverbs 11:3; Proverbs 6:17; Job 27:2–6; Psalm 25:4–5; Ephesians 6:14; John 8:32

My prayer for my child today:

41

The character trait of God that I will focus on today:
(Thank you, Lord, that you are . . .)

A promise of Scripture for today:

You will find further help in developing kids with integrity in chapter one of *Character Matters! Raising Kids with Values That Last* by John and Susan Yates.

Help! I Need a Girlfriend

We all need people in our lives to hear, encourage, and challenge us. Having a friend who is going through the same life stage as we are (or who has survived it already!) can keep us together when we feel as if we're falling apart.

Help, Lord! I need someone to talk to! On days like today I don't even know which end is up—my heart and my mind are turned inside out. It's not that there's any one particular thing wrong—it's more that everything is out of kilter and I need a friend to help me filter through this mess.

Lord, throughout your Word you give examples of great friends. I know that you are a friend to me, even one that is closer than a brother would be.* But today I need to see you "with skin on" or hear your voice on the telephone.

43

You gave Jesus's mother, Mary, and her cousin Elizabeth to each other at a pivotal point in both their lives. Both of them were expecting their first child through extraordinary circumstances!* You used their friendship and their months spent together to affirm your work in both of their lives. I need someone like this, Lord. Please bless me with a friend who gives me earnest counsel, who listens, who understands!* Sometimes just hearing the right words at the right moment can turn my day into something beautiful.*

I know that you can use girlfriends in my life to teach me things about mothering, and about yourself. Direct me to clear opportunities to meet together with other mothers who love you.* Give me friends with different strengths than mine, so that we can sharpen one another and build each other up, strengthening your body.

I long for someone who will share my silly stories and laugh and cry with me. Even though my husband wants to support me, he can never fill that girlfriend gap in my life! Lead me to the person who will hear my need and encourage my heart—or, let me be the one who offers friendship to someone else. I know that it is not good to be alone.* Sorrows are lessened and joys increased when we share them. Thank you for creating friendship, Father.*

Though you have not seen him, you love him; and even though you do not see him now, you believe in him and are filled with an inexpressible and glorious joy, for you are receiving the goal of your faith, the salvation of your souls.

1 PETER 1:8–9

Scripture references (in order of starred references in prayer): Proverbs 18:24; Luke 1:39–45; Proverbs 27:9; Proverbs 25:11; Hebrews 10:25; Genesis 2:18; Colossians 1:16

My prayer for my child today:

The character trait of God that I will focus on today:
(Thank you, Lord, that you are . . .)

A promise of Scripture for today:

See appendix 3 for resources that may help you connect with local mothering groups.

Cultivating a Heart for Christ

ore than anything we want our children to come to personal faith in Christ. We know that this is the most important decision they will ever make, and we play a crucial role in cultivating their desire to make this decision. Yet, at the same time, the decision must be their own. How do we prepare them to know Christ?

Lord, the greatest desire of my life is that my child would love you with all of his heart and walk with you all of his life. I can't make this happen. Only you can do this.

At his young age he is open to you. He's not yet hardened by cynics or swayed by peer pressure. Skeptics aren't challenging his faith. The world has yet to overwhelm him with false gods and tempting pleasures. This is a brief season in which he is most receptive to my teaching and training. I know it's a great opportunity, but I feel so inadequate!

How can I teach him about you when I still have so much to learn myself? How can I encourage him to trust you when I so often doubt? What do I say when he asks questions I can't answer?

Father, I long for him to open the door of his heart while he is young.* Father, there's a delicate balance between my telling him that he needs to know you personally and explaining to him that you want to come into his heart when he's ready to ask you. Give me the words to explain your message of salvation and the faith to leave the timing of his commitment up to you.*

Thank you for creating him and for summoning him by name!* You want him to invite you into his life even more than I want him to.* You have engraved his name in your hand.* You have a special plan for his life.* And you will always be there for him.*

Father, I'm so relieved that his relationship with you does not depend on my ability to answer his questions or even in my ability to trust you. You are so much bigger than my inadequacies. Thank you that at this very moment your Son, Jesus, is sitting at your right hand praying for my son.*

Therefore he is able to save completely those who come to God through him, because he always lives to intercede for them.

HEBREWS 7:25

Scripture references (in order of starred references in prayer): Revelation 3:20; Acts 1:7; Isaiah 43:1; John 15:16; Isaiah 49:16; Jeremiah 29:11–13; Deuteronomy 31:8; Romans 8:34

My prayer for my child today:

*The character trait of God that I will focus on today:
(Thank you, Lord, that you are . . .)*

A promise of Scripture for today:

Learning Right from Wrong

Who's right; who's wrong? What is the right thing to do? Often it depends on whom we ask and where we look for answers. Teaching our child the difference between right and wrong can be hard in a culture of blurred absolutes.

Dear Lord, your Word is so clear that there *is* a real standard of right and wrong. If I begin to teach my child the difference now, she will be more likely to know the difference when she is older. But explaining this to a young child is a challenge.

Show me practical, tangible ways that I can teach my child how to discern between right and wrong. This is something that is very important to you! Help me to be a good role model. Convict me when I blur the lines of right and wrong for my own convenience.* When I wrong her or someone else, give me the humility to confess and to ask for forgiveness. Thank you for promising to forgive all our sins!*

Father, you know all our secrets.* I ask that if my child is doing anything wrong, she will get caught so that she learns that actions have consequences. Give me the insight to know if she is not being truthful.*

Help me to be clear about consequences when she misbehaves and to be willing to follow through with punishment no matter how difficult it will be. Sometimes it seems easier for me to bail her out or let her off the hook. Instead, help me to be strong and consistent. Enable me to balance firm discipline with love and mercy. Use the consequences to teach her that actions do matter. Create within her a pure heart.* Give her a desire to seek truth and to want to do what's right in all areas of her life.*

When he, the Spirit of truth, comes, he will guide you into all truth.

JOHN 16:13

Scripture references (in order of starred references in prayer): John 16:8; 1 John 1:9; Psalm 44:21; James 1:5; Psalm 51:10; Matthew 6:33

My prayer for my child today:

The character trait of God that I will focus on today: (Thank you, Lord, that you are . . .)

A promise of Scripture for today:

Taming the Tongue

Back talk, rudeness, unacceptable language. Sometimes it's subtle; often it's "in your face." I know this is not right. It hurts. Sometimes I'm guilty. I don't want my home to be a breeding ground of verbal abuse.

Father, my child has a "mouth." He can't seem to control his tongue. He lashes out at me without even thinking. Back talk is all too common, and he says cruel things to his siblings.

You aren't surprised at the evil that comes out of his mouth *or* mine. You said so much in your Word about the tongue! You compared its power to that of a forest fire.* You warned us to keep a rein on it, to keep it from speaking evil.* You also called us to use it to bless others, even those who hurt us.* That is *hard,* Lord.

Show me how to teach my son to tame his tongue. Father, I hope I'm raising a future husband and father. I don't want him to one day wound his loved ones with his words. He must learn to control his tongue *now*. Give him the discipline to keep his mouth shut when he should.* Show me what punishment to use when he speaks in a way that is not acceptable.* Help me to be consistent. Help him to know when his words hurt others. Help us both to turn to you for help and let us see progress! We need your encouragement.

Help me to train my child to use his words in positive ways. Teach him how to compliment and to appreciate other people.* Show me specific ways in which I can help him learn how to build others up. And Father, please control my tongue today. Help me resist becoming a nag and instead show me new words to use that will encourage him.

Thank you, Father, that *your* words are always loving. You breathe your very life into us with your words.* Even the sound of your voice is majestic!*

I waited patiently for the LORD; he turned to me and heard my cry. He lifted me out of the slimy pit, out of the mud and mire; he set my feet on a rock and gave me a firm place to stand. He put a new song in my mouth, a hymn of praise to our God. Many will see and fear and put their trust in the LORD.

PSALM 40:1–3

Scripture references (in order of starred references in prayer): James 3:5–6; James 1:26; Romans 12:14; Proverbs 11:12; Psalm 34:13; 1 Peter 3:8–9; Genesis 1:26; Psalm 29:4

My prayer for my child today:

*The character trait of God that I will focus on today:
(Thank you, Lord, that you are . . .)*

A promise of Scripture for today:

Overcoming the Past

None of us knows innately how to be a good parent. Sometimes our personal history might handicap us. Even if we have not had good role models in parenting, or if we have messed things up ourselves, God is bigger than all of our inadequacies.

Dear Lord, sometimes I take a hard look at myself and I am frightened that I am a mother. I don't know what I'm doing—really, I don't. Many of my childhood experiences were pleasant, but there are some that pain me to recall. There are scars on my heart, and I am afraid that I will repeat mistakes I experienced as a child. I feel ill equipped and frightened that I will hurt my child in some way.

Your Word promises me that you will guide me through this. You will show me one step at a time, as if a light were shining on my path.* Lord, illumine me. Shine through me into the dark places that I don't know how to handle. Give me wisdom that can only come from you.

I have habits from my sinful past that are not pleasing to you. Please make these obvious to me (as gently as possible, Lord) and help me to know how to get rid of them.* I know that I am a forgiven, new creation because I am in you and you are in me.* Free me from the mistakes of my own past—and show me clearly any unhealthy family habits that need to be broken with my generation. I want to start a new tradition of loving you and living for you. Give me the courage to make positive changes in my life, for my children's sake.

Help me to put behind the former things, getting rid of the ones that need to be disposed of. Thank you that you do not remember my sin but cast it as far from me as the east is from the west.* I know you are doing something new in my life, and I see it before my eyes daily in this little child you have given me.

Father, I long to be the first of many generations of healthy families who love you. I ask you to pour out your blessings, showering your love on this new generation and on those to come.*

This is what the LORD says—he who made a way through the sea, a path through the mighty waters. . . . "Forget the former things; do not dwell on the past. See, I am doing a new thing! Now it springs up; do you not perceive it? I am making a way in the desert and streams in the wasteland."

ISAIAH 43:16, 18–19

Scripture references (in order of starred references in prayer): Psalm 119:105; Jeremiah 10:24; 2 Corinthians 5:17; Psalm 103:12; Exodus 20:6

My prayer for my child today:

*The character trait of God that I will focus on today:
(Thank you, Lord, that you are . . .)*

A promise of Scripture for today:

This Child Belongs to God

Though we are the parents of our children, they ultimately belong to God. He has given them to us only for a brief time. How do we balance the authority we have as their parents with the need to fully surrender them to God's plan for their lives?

Lord, I prayed about having children long before this child was ever conceived.* You answered, and you brought us a child in your time. Thank you! I am grateful and humbled that you have entrusted this little person to me. I am awed by the responsibility of raising him.

I understand, Father, that you are God and I am not. I struggle with this, though, wanting to control every aspect of my child's life—for his own good. But you have told me in your Word that it is not my plans that prevail but yours.*

57

I want *you* to have the ultimate authority in my child's life. I want him to be fully *yours*, though I admit that I struggle with this deep in my heart.

I give my child to you. I know that Mary and Joseph took Jesus to the temple when he was a newborn to present him to you, heavenly Father.* When Hannah's long-awaited son Samuel was three years old, she took him to the temple too. In the same way, Father, I give my child to you, for his whole life.* I give you ultimate authority and responsibility for him. Lead him, guide him, have your way in his life.

I know there will be days when I want to "take him back"— when I want to protect him from pain that you intend to use for good, or when I selfishly want to be more important to him than you are. Lord, remind me over and over that you love him more than I do.* Your will in his life is perfect, even when it seems different from what *I* want for him. Help me this day to entrust him into your tender arms.

You are worthy, our Lord and God, to receive glory and honor and power, for you created all things, and by your will they were created and have their being.

REVELATION 4:11

Scripture references (in order of starred references in prayer): 1 Samuel 1:27; Proverbs 19:21; Luke 2:22–23; 1 Samuel 1:28; Exodus 15:13

My prayer for my child today:

The character trait of God that I will focus on today: (Thank you, Lord, that you are . . .)

A promise of Scripture for today:

In our family, we have made it a tradition to "offer our child back to God" shortly after he (or she) is born. My husband and I set aside a time of prayer especially for the baby—to "present" him to God. We give thanks for this child, dedicating him, and ourselves, to the Lord. This serves as a clear reminder to us that this child, though given to our keeping for a time, truly belongs to God. You may choose to do this when the baby is eight days old (based on the traditional time frame for circumcision) or within a few months of his birth (based on traditional rites of purification). For us, this is a private family ceremony and does not replace the traditions within our larger church body.

Getting to Know You

Our children are individuals—they are their own little selves. They may reflect our personality or look like their daddy, but they are created to be unique. How can I affirm and encourage the special person God created my child to be?

Lord, I'm flattered when people say, "Your daughter looks just like you!" This is definitely a compliment for me, but I'm not so sure how *she* feels about it! I want my child to resemble me in *some* ways. She sure doesn't seem like me in many other respects! Sometimes I don't quite understand her perspective on the world, and I get frustrated that she doesn't go about things in the way I would.

Forgive me, Father, for expecting my child to be just like

60

me. I know that one of me in this world is probably plenty! Forgive me for comparing my child to her siblings or to other children. When you look at her, you see only her, and *you are pleased* with your creation.

My desire, Lord, is to see this child you have made in the way that you see her. You are not distracted by appearances but you look only at her heart.* You have called her by name and she is yours.* Help me to be a good student of my daughter.* Give me eyes to see the gifts you have given her that set her apart from others. Help her to use these for your glory. Thank you for making her different from me!* Show me today tangible ways to encourage her as she pursues interests that suit *her*.

Stop me when I try to mold my daughter into a miniature me. Help me give her room to breathe and to discover who she is. And while you're at it, Lord, please teach me something new about myself. Remind both of us that we are your beloveds and that you take great delight in us!*

Now the Lord is the Spirit, and where the Spirit of the Lord is, there is freedom. And we, who with unveiled faces all reflect the Lord's glory, are being transformed into his likeness with ever-increasing glory, which comes from the Lord, who is the Spirit.

2 CORINTHIANS 3:17–18

Scripture references (in order of starred references in prayer): 1 Samuel 16:7; Isaiah 43:1; 1 Corinthians 12:18–19; 1 Corinthians 12:4, 7; Song of Songs 7:6

My prayer for my child today:

61

*The character trait of God that I will focus on today:
(Thank you, Lord, that you are . . .)*

A promise of Scripture for today:

Unrealistic Expectations?

Expectations can be a weighty burden. Sometimes we put them on ourselves; other times they are spoken by those we love and want desperately to please. The more we try to live up to them, the more we realize we can't.

Father, I come from a great family. I had good role models and a secure childhood. Mom and Dad weren't perfect, but they gave us a great foundation. But sometimes I feel burdened by expectations—my own, my parents', my peers'. I don't know if I can live up to them!

Father, you know I put pressure on myself by saying, *You have no excuses; you should be able to do this parenting thing. You are a capable person. After all, you've had good role models, been to parenting seminars, and read all the best books.*

Whenever I lose my temper or don't have an answer for a hurt child or let my husband down, I feel like a failure. Guilt overwhelms me because I think *I* should know better.

Could it be that pride is rearing its ugly face once again? Could it be that my expectations of myself are unreasonable?

Father, forgive me. It *is* my pride, clothed in unrealistic expectations. I am sinful, and apart from you I can do nothing.* My heritage is a blessing. It is not a guarantee. Even doing "all the right things" will not guarantee that my children will turn out right. I need you just as much as the next person. I cannot do this in my own strength. I am failing, and in the process I am condemning myself.

Thank you that you do not condemn me.* Thank you that you know I am just dust!* You know my frailty,* and your love for me isn't dependent on my being a good mother or a good wife or a good friend. You love me just because I am your child.*

Father, I do praise you for my heritage. I thank you for parents who loved you and who spoke of you to me. You chose this family of origin for me, and I am so thankful. Keep me grateful and not burdened.

Father, I pray that you would continue the work in our family that you began generations ago. I know you long for each of my children and grandchildren to have a deep love for you and a desire to walk with you all their days. I ask that not one would be lost until you come again.

"As for me, this is my covenant with them," says the LORD. "My Spirit, who is on you, and my words that I have put in your mouth will not depart from your mouth, or from the mouths of your children, or from the mouths of their descendants from this time on and forever," says the LORD.

ISAIAH 59:21

64

*Scripture references (in order of starred references in prayer):
John 15:5; John 3:18; Psalm 103:14; Matthew 26:41; Psalm
145:8–9*

My prayer for my child today:

*The character trait of God that I will focus on today:
(Thank you, Lord, that you are . . .)*

A promise of Scripture for today:

Considering Others

I n our "me-oriented" culture it's easy to raise self-centered kids. But a self-centered person will never be happy or satisfied. Instead God calls us to consider others as more important than ourselves.

Father, my child is so self-centered. I feel as if I'm always catering to him. His demands are quickly becoming, "Satisfy me, meet my needs, make me happy, entertain me, please me." If things don't go his way, everyone around him finds out real fast! I realize that at his age I still have to do many things for him, but I also know that as he is growing up I have to teach him that the world does not revolve around him.

I long for him to mature into an adult who is more "others-centered" than "me-centered." I know I need to train him to think of others while he is young.

Father, in your great commandment you called us to love you with all our heart, mind, and soul and our neighbor as ourselves.* You demonstrated this when you gave your only Son for us.* You are a giving God. You gave freely without expectation of anything in return. And what you got in return was horrible rejection. Your nature is perfectly, lovingly, "others-centered."

Your apostle Paul reminds us not to think of ourselves more highly than we ought to* and to do nothing out of selfish ambition or vain conceit but in humility to consider others better than ourselves.*

Father, this doesn't come naturally. My child is bombarded with advertisements that tell him what he needs to have to be happy. I too feel pressured to make sure he is happy.

Show me how to teach him to think of others. Help me teach him to ask himself, "What are their needs? How can I care for them?" Give my child eyes to notice the elderly, the sad child in his class, the kid no one plays with at recess. Show us specific ways he can demonstrate love to others. Show me how we can practice this together as a family.

He has showed you, O man, what is good. And what does the LORD require of you? To act justly and to love mercy and to walk humbly with your God.

MICAH 6:8

Scripture references (in order of starred references in prayer): Matthew 22:37–39; John 3:16; Romans 12:3; Philippians 2:3–4

My prayer for my child today:

The character trait of God that I will focus on today:
(Thank you, Lord, that you are . . .)

A promise of Scripture for today:

Too Many Choices

L ife is too full. We feel as if we're racing from one event to another. There are so many good options for ways in which our children can spend their time! Is the best mother the one whose kids are the busiest?

Father, life is too full! I feel as if I live in the car. There are too many activities to choose from! It wouldn't be so hard if the choices were between good and evil, but they are all good. There's a subtle pressure that seems to say, *whoever's child is the most involved is the best parent.*

I know this isn't true! Yet, it's so easy to fall into the trap of overcommitment. And it only makes me feel stressed. Lord, I know that in the long run it is more important to say no to many of these things. It's my job to help my children draw the line. All these activities only earn us trophies that will one day collect dust on closet shelves. You want us to be putting our energies into things that will last a lifetime—like our family friendships. I do want to nurture friendships rather than collect trophies.

I need your help, God. When young King Solomon asked for a discerning heart* to govern your people, his request pleased you and you gave it to him.* Show me what to say yes to and what to postpone or say no to. Speak your truth to me about all my options, so I may know what is good and right for our family. Free me from the burden of all the "shoulds" and "coulds."

Thank you for showing me that there are seasons in life.* We don't have to do it all in any one season. Show me the things I need to save for another season instead of trying to add to our lives right now. Give me a long-range perspective as I make difficult choices. Give me the courage to stand firm even when my child doesn't like my decision.

Thank you for caring about things like activities and opportunities. Thank you for promising that you will give me the wisdom to make wise choices.*

I love the LORD, for he heard my voice; he heard my cry for mercy. Because he turned his ear to me, I will call on him as long as I live.

PSALM 116:1–2

Scripture references (in order of starred references in prayer): 1 Kings 3:7–12; 1 Chronicles 22:11–12; Ecclesiastes 3:1; James 1:5

My prayer for my child today:

The character trait of God that I will focus on today:
(Thank you, Lord, that you are . . .)

A promise of Scripture for today:

Teachers and Caregivers

From teachers to babysitters, it is frightening to leave our children in the care of other people. We have so little control over what happens when we're not around! What if they mistreat them?

Dear God, I know my child so well. I understand how he is made and what his needs are. But I have to trust other people with him! I have to release him to the care of teachers, babysitters, and child-care centers. This frightens me!

What if the babysitter doesn't pay close enough attention and something terrible happens? What if the teacher hurts my son's feelings? He is so tenderhearted, and she might not realize that! What if something scary happens at a friend's house? What if the people I leave my child with are in some way unsafe or not able to adequately care for him?

Please free me from this fear, Lord. Give me your peace.* Father, hide my child in the shadow of your wings.* Protect him by the power of your name, wherever he is at this very moment.* Give my child discernment and awareness—let him tell me quickly if there is ever anything unsafe about his situation. Keep my child from harm at the hands of those he trusts.

Give us godly caregivers. Specifically I pray for _____ and _____. Bless them as they care for my child today. Give them supernatural patience and gentle understanding.* Give them wisdom as they correct and guide my child.* Help them to lead my child in paths of righteousness.*

I ask that today you would enable his teacher to encourage him to persevere at something he finds difficult, such as _____. I know that it delights you when I pray specifically. Thank you that you have a tender heart toward all children and that you care deeply about the well-being of my child.*

Ask and it will be given to you; seek and you will find; knock and the door will be opened to you. For everyone who asks receives; he who seeks finds; and to him who knocks, the door will be opened. . . . How much more will your Father in heaven give good gifts to those who ask him!
MATTHEW 7:7–8, 11

Scripture references (in order of starred references in prayer): John 14:27; Psalm 17:8; John 17:11; Ephesians 4:2; Proverbs 29:15; Psalm 23:3; Mark 10:13–16

My prayer for my child today:

The character trait of God that I will focus on today:
(Thank you, Lord, that you are . . .)

A promise of Scripture for today:

My Child's Friends

Friend/enemy; loyalty/rejection. . . . Even a young child wields the power to encourage or to hurt a tender heart. And those cliques. I didn't think they started until the kids got bigger! Handling our child's friendships is a sensitive issue.

Lord, my daughter was in tears today over whom to invite to her birthday party. One little girl told her that if she invited a certain child, then *she* wouldn't come to the party. Honestly, I wanted to slap that child and scratch her off the list, but that wouldn't be too godly, now would it? Sometimes I have to remind myself that I'm the parent here, not the child!

God, I'm thankful I can be honest with you about my feelings! I am finding children's friendships to be so tricky! I want my daughter to be the one who cares for everyone, *especially* the unlovely. But the little girl that still lives inside of me wants my daughter to be loved by everyone. I cringe when I see her eagerly sidle up to the "popular" girl who then proceeds to ignore her. Sometimes I'm even more crushed than she is by the social bruises.

Father, I am asking for your wisdom. How do I help my child learn to handle rejection now and prepare her to survive it for the rest of her life? How do I do this when I struggle with it myself?

You were mocked and rejected. You know what it's like to be forsaken by people you *thought* were your faithful friends.* You were hurt, but you forgave and you still had compassion.*   I long for this for my child. Show me ways to model this to her so she can understand.

I know I can't control every aspect of my daughter's relationships, Lord. But I pray that you would help me guide her in the direction of good friends when it is appropriate to do so. Put a little girl in her life that comes from a family who knows you. Guard her heart.* Protect her from friends who will be untrue or who will be a bad influence. Give us both the discernment to know which relationships *not* to pursue. And when her little heart is hurt, help me to validate her feelings with compassion and yet not overreact. Equip me with words that will enable her to choose to show kindness to others no matter how they are behaving toward her.*

Thank you, Father, for the joy that my child will find in friendships throughout her life. Thank you that these relationships, like all good things, come from you.

His divine power has given us everything we need for life and godliness through our knowledge of him who called us by his own glory and goodness. Through these he has given us his very great and precious promises.

2 PETER 1:3–4

Scripture references (in order of starred references in prayer):
Matthew 26:14–16, 40; Luke 23:34; Proverbs 4:23; Matthew
5:39–42

My prayer for my child today:

The character trait of God that I will focus on today:
(Thank you, Lord, that you are . . .)

A promise of Scripture for today:

Waiting

Y ou'll just have to wait" is such a hard phrase. There is nothing in us—or our children—that likes to wait. We want answers now. We want guidance now. We want things to be fixed now. Waiting hurts.

O Lord, today I feel stuck. I can't hear you. I need answers. I don't know what to do. I feel helpless. I want to help my child, but I don't know how.

I feel as if I'm on "hold." I'm calling out to you, but I can't hear your answers. Could it be that I have to learn to wait? Could it be that my child has to learn to wait? I don't like to wait, Father. I live in an instant society. I expect you to work instantly too. I know a lot of life is waiting. But it's so hard. It hurts to watch my child suffer. What if he thinks you don't care?

But you *do* care, Lord.* It's good for my child to learn to wait while he's young.* If he learns to wait for little things now, he'll be more likely to wait for big things when he's an adult. Sometimes I have the power to fix things for him *right now*. But that isn't always wise. Show me when I should *not* satisfy his desires and instead teach him to wait. Show me how to encourage my child to maintain a sensitive heart and open ears to you in the "waiting."

There are also times, Lord, when I don't know what to do and *I* am forced to wait. I cry out to you and silence is all I hear. And so I wait, often impatiently! Thank you that you are at work even when I *don't* get a quick answer or see any evidence of a solution.* I know that you do what is best, not necessarily what is fast. You are working while I am waiting.*

When we are in times of waiting, speak to both of us and help us come to know you in a deeper, perhaps unexpected, way. Thank you for promising that you can use everything— even waiting—for good in our lives.*

You will keep in perfect peace him whose mind is steadfast, because he trusts in you.

ISAIAH 26:3

Scripture references (in order of starred references in prayer): Isaiah 30:18; Psalm 27:14; Isaiah 55:8–9; Isaiah 30:18; Romans 8:28

My prayer for my child today:

The character trait of God that I will focus on today:
(Thank you, Lord, that you are . . .)

A promise of Scripture for today:

Forgiveness

You and I are going to fail. We are going to hurt each other and so are our children. Our sin is the reason Christ died on the cross. He waits to forgive us. But we have to ask him and each other. Forgiveness could be the most important ingredient in the family.

Father, you know I just got really angry with my daughter over a fight she was having with her brother. I was too tired to find out what really happened. I lashed out at her with ugly words. Now, I've found out that none of it was her fault! She's crying, I'm crying, and I've blown it again.

Lord, I need to apologize and ask her to forgive me for my harsh words. But it's so hard. After all, I'm the mom and I'd like to add "but you should have . . ." or "but you shouldn't have . . ." And it's embarrassing. I don't feel like asking her to forgive me. I'd rather just carry on.

It isn't just this time, Lord. I do the same with my husband too. Times when I say something I shouldn't; times I intentionally hurt him. In those times I need to ask his forgiveness as well. When it's an accident, it might be enough to say "I'm sorry," but often it's not. When I have to ask forgiveness it's completely different—it demands a response. The person I've hurt has to decide whether or not to forgive. Father, I know I can't wait until I feel like it to ask for forgiveness. I need to do it now, out of obedience. You have told me to confess my sins and ask for forgiveness*—and then wait, trusting in you to bring healing to the wounded emotions.* Your healing process can't begin until I ask for forgiveness.*

Father, give me courage as I try to obey you. Little eyes are watching me. Help me to teach my children to ask for forgiveness and to give it. I want all their relationships to be characterized by grace, and they need to begin learning this now.

Thank you for loving us despite the condition of our hearts.* You called King David "a man after your own heart" even though he committed many grievous sins. You are never shocked by my actions or my child's behavior. Our sorrow over sin pleases you, and you offer complete forgiveness.* And Lord, thank you that when you do forgive, you cast our sins far away and you choose never to remember them.*

As far as the east is from the west, so far has he removed our transgressions from us.

PSALM 103:12

Scripture references (in order of starred references in prayer): Psalm 66:18–20; 1 John 1:8–10; James 5:13–16; 2 Chronicles 6:30; Psalm 51:17; Isaiah 43:25

My prayer for my child today:

The character trait of God that I will focus on today:
(Thank you, Lord, that you are . . .)

A promise of Scripture for today:

Health Matters

One of the hardest things about parenting is not knowing. We don't always know what is best for our children or what is wrong when they are hurting. Health issues can seem so scary and confusing. Thank goodness we know the One who does know!

Lord, the baby is sick again.

He's lying on the floor screaming in pain I can't decipher. The pediatrician tells me one thing ("tubes in the ears—and quick!"); my friend tells me another ("go homeopathic!"). Everyone has an answer and none of them seems to be the right one. I wish my baby could tell me what's wrong.

I have so many fears and questions about my child's health. How will I know if something is really wrong? What if I miss the signs? What if I overreact and rush him to the hospital for something minor? What if he chokes? What if he contracts a fatal illness?

Please protect the health of my child, Father. You know his little frame; you know what he is made of.* You knit him together within the womb, fearfully and wonderfully.* You crafted every part of him. When he hurts, you hurt. You are also the healer, Father.* You want us to ask you for things.* Lord, you have the power to heal the sick and raise the dead.* I ask that you use that power to heal my child today, and in your goodness protect his body from future harm.

Give me the discernment to know when my child is really sick, and when he just needs a little extra love. Give our doctors a personal interest in the health of my child, and make them keenly observant. When I face fears and medical questions I don't understand, give me your peace that passes understanding.* Give your wisdom as I make decisions. Protect our schools, churches, and child-care centers from outbreaks of contagious disease.

Thank you that you don't find my fears for my child's health silly or unreasonable but that you care about those things too. I trust you, Lord. I know that no one who puts their trust in you will ever be put to shame.*

Blessed is the man who trusts in the LORD, whose confidence is in him. He will be like a tree planted by the water that sends out its roots by the stream. It does not fear when heat comes; its leaves are always green. It has no worries in a year of drought and never fails to bear fruit. . . . Heal me, O LORD, and I will be healed; save me and I will be saved, for you are the one I praise.

JEREMIAH 17:7–8, 14

Scripture references (in order of starred references in prayer): Psalm 103:14; Psalm 139:13–14; Exodus 15:26; Matthew 7:7; Luke 8:40–55; Philippians 4:7; Psalm 25:2–3

My prayer for my child today:

*The character trait of God that I will focus on today:
(Thank you, Lord, that you are . . .)*

A promise of Scripture for today:

A House of Joy

We all want our homes to be places where people feel loved and welcomed. But that just doesn't happen naturally. As mothers we often have to be the ones who deliberately set the tone in our homes.

I think the saying is true, God, that "if Mama ain't happy, ain't nobody happy." I'm tempted to grumble, but today, with your help, I am choosing to be joyful. I want others to see a gentleness* in me that reminds them you are near. Bring to mind today things that are lovely and praiseworthy,* especially if I start to get a case of self-pity. I don't want to be fake or insincere—that is why I'm relying on you! I know that I control much of the atmosphere in this home, and I want this place to be characterized by joy!

Let's build a new house, Lord. I don't mean a physical structure, but let's build this home with wisdom, understanding, and knowledge, so that one day it will be filled with rare and beautiful treasures—hearts full of you.* When someone walks in my front door, let them be so attracted by your warmth that they don't even see the dirt and dust. Let our home be a place of transformation* where my children and our friends can be at peace and full of laughter (and if you want to transform all this clutter, too, please feel free!). Make this a place where people want to be—especially my children's friends. Give our family the sincerity to rejoice with those who are glad and to mourn alongside those who cry.* And then, Lord, I ask boldly that you transform mourning into gladness in this home.*

Thank you for living in me and for inhabiting this home! Daily fill this place with your spirit of love, joy, and peace.* Let us rejoice and be glad in you* because you are our constant hope, no matter what life throws our way. I know life is hard, but don't let me be lacking in zeal. Keep me spiritually fervent!*

The LORD is my strength and my song; he has become my salvation. He is my God, and I will praise him, my father's God, and I will exalt him.

EXODUS 15:2

Scripture references (in order of starred references in prayer): Philippians 4:5; Philippians 4:8; Proverbs 24:3–4; Romans 12:2; Romans 12:15; Jeremiah 31:13; Galatians 5:22; Psalm 118:24; Romans 12:11

My prayer for my child today:

The character trait of God that I will focus on today:
(Thank you, Lord, that you are . . .)

A promise of Scripture for today:

DAY 26

The Discipline Dilemma

D iscipline is one of the most confusing issues in parenting. Our parents may have one approach, our friends another, and we may disagree with our spouse! How do we decide what is right?

Father, I don't know what my approach to discipline should be. Sometimes I fear I'm too firm, and other times I'm too lenient. It's hard to be consistent, especially when the kids try to play me against my husband! My strong-willed child needs a firm hand, and when he's disciplined he makes life miserable for all of us. Some days I don't want to deal with his tantrums, so I let them go. My inconsistency isn't helpful.

You understand my frustration, Father. Adam and Eve did not obey you; your instruction was for their good, but they wanted their own way. How like my children! How like me! Their disobedience had dire consequences, even for us.* It must break your heart when we do not obey you.

I know it's important to teach my child to obey me, Father. He can feel my hugs and hear me tell him that I love him. Yet, I am trying to teach him that you love him too—and that he ultimately must learn to obey you. This is so hard to convey to a child who can't see you. Don't let me give up! How can I expect him to obey you if I have not taught him to obey me?*

Father, help me with this overwhelming task. Show me how to balance love and discipline.* Help my spouse and me to know what strategies are best for our child and to stick with them with fair measures of firmness and grace. Give us perseverance and consistency. Remind us to praise our child for the things he does right.*

Lord, your Word is full of your thoughts about discipline. You discipline those you love, because love and discipline go hand in hand.* Help me receive your discipline of me, Father.

God disciplines us for our good, that we may share in his holiness. No discipline seems pleasant at the time, but painful. Later on, however, it produces a harvest of righteousness and peace for those who have been trained by it.

HEBREWS 12:10–11

Scripture references (in order of starred references in prayer): Genesis 3; Deuteronomy 32:46-47; 2 Timothy 4:2; Hebrews 3:13; Proverbs 3:11–12

My prayer for my child today:

91

The character trait of God that I will focus on today:
(Thank you, Lord, that you are . . .)

A promise of Scripture for today:

For help in determining a discipline strategy, see chapter six in *And Then I Had Kids: Encouragement for Mothers of Young Children* by Susan Alexander Yates. If you are a single parent, it will be helpful to meet with a couple whose children are approximately the same age as yours and work on a philosophy together.

Fear—Theirs and Mine

Dark rooms, fierce animals, loud noises—so many things can frighten my child. New things, even good things, can also evoke fear: a new babysitter, the first day of school, or trying a new sport. Some of my child's fears seem silly to me, but then many of my fears must seem unnecessary to God. My child and I both need help!

Father, so many of my child's fears are unnecessary. As his parent I know he's going to be okay. And yet in his fears I see my own. I fear he'll be rejected at school or have an accident. And when I let my mind wander, I fear another terrorist attack, the loss of a job, a financial crisis, or the death of someone I love. It is easier to give more weight to my fears than to his. And fear can paralyze.

Father, help me to remember that you love me with a Father's love. You do not want me to live in fear but to live

93

in the knowledge that you are in charge and that you will always be with me.* My love and my desire to protect my child is nothing compared to the love and the desire you have to protect him and me. Your love and your power are far greater than anything I could ever imagine.*

When my child is afraid, help me to teach him to turn to you.* Show me how to give him the confidence to take good risks. Help him to become a man of courage like Joshua was.*

This world will never be safe. I cannot protect my child from all dangers. But I can tell him about you, his heavenly Father, who loves him even more than I do. You have even numbered the hairs on his little head.* You are the only one who will never leave him.* You can overcome his fears (and mine) with your peace, a peace so powerful that it cannot be explained.*

We can have confidence in your promise that one day we will be in heaven with you.* We will be completely safe. No one and nothing can take that assurance away.

When I said, "My foot is slipping," your love, O LORD, supported me. When anxiety was great within me, your consolation brought joy to my soul.

PSALM 94:18–19

Scripture references (in order of starred references in prayer): Romans 8:15–17; Ephesians 1:18–20; Psalm 56:3–4; Joshua 1:9; Matthew 10:29–31; Deuteronomy 31:6; Philippians 4:6–7; 1 John 5:13

My prayer for my child today:

The character trait of God that I will focus on today:
(Thank you, Lord, that you are . . .)

A promise of Scripture for today:

A Grateful Heart

Needs and demands are everywhere in our homes. We have lists to accomplish and deadlines to meet. And there are all those things we want for our children. It is easy to become so busy "doing" that we neglect the obvious—what God has already done!

Father, it's so easy for me to get bogged down by the needs in my household. I get overwhelmed with all the things I need to do—and that I ask you to do—that I forget all that you have already done for me! How often I forget to say "thank you."

I'm so much like my child. He always seems to want something! Yet rarely does he thank me for something that I have done for him. Most of the time he simply takes me for granted and fails to notice all I do. How I long to hear the words "Thanks, Mom! You're the best!" What joy that would bring to my heart.

Lord, you long for your children to praise you too!* You don't need our praise, but you delight in it. You give us good gifts gladly, with no expectation of return, yet what joy it would bring you if we did thank you. You healed ten lepers, Lord, and only one returned to praise and thank you.* I want to be like that one—I want my life to be a thank offering to you! And I desire to raise children with thankful hearts as well, Lord.

You have told us in your Word that we should give thanks continually.* When I thank you, I am reminded that you are my provider and that I must continually rely on you. I don't always feel like thanking you when things are hard—but I will try to, Father.

Let me start by saying "thank you" for being the one who makes me glad.* You sustain me, you meet my needs, and you bring me great joy! Lord, I also thank you for who you are. You are my Abba, Father.* You are the King of Kings,* the one in whom there is no darkness at all,* the one who loves me the most,* the one who is always good.*

Father, as I learn to praise you more, I ask that this habit would trickle down into my relationships with others. Remind me to affirm other people. As I do this, show me how to train my child in practicing thankfulness. Today, reveal to us a person we can actively appreciate. Show us someone we can thank in a special way.

Please, Father, make this house a home full of thankful people!

For the LORD takes delight in his people; he crowns the humble with salvation. Let the saints rejoice in this honor and sing for joy on their beds.

PSALM 149:4–5

Scripture references (in order of starred references in prayer): 1 Chronicles 16:25; Luke 17:11–19; 1 Thessalonians 5:17–18;

Psalm 21:6; Romans 8:15; 1 Timothy 6:15; 1 John 1:5; John 3:16; Psalm 34:8

My prayer for my child today:

The character trait of God that I will focus on today: (Thank you, Lord, that you are . . .)

A promise of Scripture for today:

Marriage?
What Marriage?

D ay in and day out we live in reaction to whatever is going on with our children. They consume most of our time. It's easy to put our marriage "on hold." But this is dangerous, and for the sake of our children we must not fall into this trap.

Lord, how am I supposed to find time for my husband in the midst of everything else? He's busy. I'm exhausted. By the time we get the kids to bed we're too numb to make conversation, let alone make love! Too often I feel as if I'm failing as a wife, but I feel disappointed in him too. How easy it would be just to let our relationship slide. I keep thinking we'll work on our marriage "when life calms down." But life won't calm down; it will only get more complicated.

Father, my relationship with my husband has to be the first priority after my relationship with you. It feels so natural to let the kids come first. Their demands are always immediate! This puts our marriage in second place, and in the long run that will hurt us all. Much of our children's security comes from knowing Mom and Dad love each other, and they are learning how to be a husband or wife as they watch us. What a scary thought! Help us to keep this in mind and be careful, living wisely while our children watch.*

Forgive me, Lord, when I focus on what bothers me about my husband.* When I start to do this, remind me of my own faults!* Instead, I want to thank you for these two traits I appreciate in him: _____ and _____. I ask you to enable me to greet him with joy when he comes home today. Give me words to affirm and honor him for the things he does right. Give us wisdom to figure out how to get some time alone together on a regular basis.* Give me the creativity and energy to put some spark back into our relationship. I feel I have so little to offer, Lord, so I'm relying on you! I thank you that you are the cord that binds the two of us together and that you are *for* our marriage. With your strength, we will not be overpowered.*

I will give you a new heart and put a new spirit in you; I will remove from you your heart of stone and give you a heart of flesh. And I will put my Spirit in you and move you to follow my decrees and be careful to keep my laws.

EZEKIEL 36:26–27

Scripture references (in order of starred references in prayer): Ephesians 5:15; Proverbs 14:1; Psalm 139:24; Song of Songs 1:4; Ecclesiastes 4:9–12

My prayer for my child today:

The character trait of God that I will focus on today:
(Thank you, Lord, that you are . . .)

A promise of Scripture for today:

If you are a single parent, you may find that the prayer on Day 30 is more suited to your needs.

DAY 30

I'm All Alone

Many women feel they are parenting in a vacuum. They may be single mothers, wives whose husbands are always traveling, or alone in a marriage that is not a partnership of faith. At some point, all of us feel alone and insufficient in our mothering.

Lord, today I come before you feeling small and afraid. I feel like a frail reed, bending in the breeze almost to the breaking point. I am trying desperately hard to be the best mother I can be, but I don't see how I can do this on my own. Some days I want to give up. I fear my children will suffer because they lack so many things I can't provide, both physically and emotionally.

Send me your Spirit, Father. Help me. Help my children. You have promised that your grace is all sufficient and that your power is made perfect in weakness.* Send us your power and your grace today.

I love the stories of your magnificent provision. You took a small boy's lunch—only a portion of bread and fish—and made it feed five thousand people, with a dozen bushels left over.* You are extravagant in your generosity! Lord, all I have to offer is a few "small fish." Take my meager efforts and multiply them on behalf of my children, Father! Provide for them in ways that I can't even imagine.* Provide male role models for my children. Give me other adults to walk alongside me in parenting—to help me in my areas of weakness and to strengthen our family. You are the champion of orphans and widows,* you delight in providing good things,* and you use your body, the church, on this earth to show your provision. Let my children learn to call you "Father" as they see the ways that you meet our needs and show your love again and again.

Thank you, Father, that you hear my requests. You encourage me; you listen to my cries.* And Father, even though I feel so alone, you are with me. You will never leave me or forsake me.* You are my helper, so I will not be afraid!* You began a good work in me and my children, and you will carry it on to completion until the day of Christ Jesus.*

This is what God the LORD says—he who created the heavens and stretched them out, who spread out the earth and all that comes out of it, who gives breath to its people, and life to those who walk on it: "I, the LORD, have called you in righteousness; I will take hold of your hand."

ISAIAH 42:5–6

Scripture references (in order of starred references in prayer): 2 Corinthians 12:9; John 6:1–13; Ephesians 3:20; James 1:27; Matthew 7:11; Psalm 10:17; Joshua 1:5; Hebrews 13:6; Philippians 1:6

My prayer for my child today:

The character trait of God that I will focus on today:
(Thank you, Lord, that you are . . .)

A promise of Scripture for today:

DAY 31

Be Still?

A child is the perfect example of the physical law stating "an object in motion will stay in motion . . ." and thus I am in perpetual motion as well! Finding spaces of quiet is like fighting the gravitational force. Yet—our souls crave this stillness.

If I could just sit still, Lord! If I sat still too long though, I'd have one child up a tree and another swinging from the chandelier. And if I let myself rest, I might fall asleep and never wake up! But there is a small, dusty corner of myself that craves stillness and quiet and your presence. Right at this very moment I will be still and know that you are God.* Quiet me with your love, O Lord.*

I long to hear you, Father. I am glad that sometimes your voice thunders majestically,* because otherwise I might not hear it above the racket in my home! Your voice has the power to still a storm to a whisper and to hush the roaring waves of the sea.* Quiet the storms in my life, Lord. Teach me to listen to you without distraction.

Show me how to rest. You were far busier than I, yet you rested when you were weary.* Let me be an example to my children in this. You have said that in repentance and rest is our salvation, in quietness and trust is our strength.* I so often choose to have none of this, finding it easier to scurry around as if the world depended on me! Forgive me, Father. You have said that you long to be gracious to me and that I will be blessed if I am willing to wait.* Right now I am choosing to wait for you—for whatever you have in store for me and my children today.

Surprise me with stillness today, Lord! Maybe I'll find it while waiting in line or in some other unexpected place. Give me an awareness of your gentle voice. Cultivate in me the unfading beauty of a gentle and quiet spirit, of such great worth in your eyes* so that even in the midst of life's noise, I can sense your calming presence.

Let us acknowledge the LORD; let us press on to acknowledge him. As surely as the sun rises, he will appear; he will come to us like the winter rains, like the spring rains that water the earth.

HOSEA 6:3

Scripture references (in order of starred references in prayer): Psalm 46:10; Zephaniah 3:17; Job 37:4; Psalm 107:29; Mark 6:31; Isaiah 30:15; Isaiah 30:18; 1 Peter 3:4

My prayer for my child today:

The character trait of God that I will focus on today:
(Thank you, Lord, that you are . . .)

A promise of Scripture for today:

Epilogue

I have something really important to tell you.

You are doing a great job!

Right now, you probably don't feel like it. In fact, you may feel more like a failure than a good mother. If so, you are in good company. And you are normal!

When Allison had just turned seven and our boys were two and four, we were surprised with twin girls! Six weeks after the twins were born we moved from Pennsylvania to northern Virginia. I had no friends, no help, and no family near by. The twins were colicky so I was constantly sleep deprived. In those days I didn't feel like a very good mother. I didn't feel like a good wife either, and I certainly wasn't "doing anything for God." I was just plain exhausted, discouraged, and defeated.

My saving grace came in the form of my next-door neighbor, Edith. A widow in her seventies, Edith lived alone. She had a quiet and gentle spirit. She had grown children and several grandchildren.

I can't tell you how many times I'd run out my front door, often barefoot or in my pj's, cross the wet grass, and knock on Edith's door. When she opened the door, I'd burst into tears.

"Edith, I'm the worst mother in the world. I'm not even a good wife. No matter how hard I try, the kids don't behave. I say things I shouldn't. I keep doing so many things wrong!"

Edith would put her arms around me and pull me into her living room and sit down with me on her well-worn couch and say, "Susan, you are not a bad mother. You are not a bad wife. You are doing a good job. It's just this season in your life. It's overwhelming. You will be all right. Your kids will be just fine. God is patient, and he's at work even if you can't see it right now."

What Edith gave me was *perspective*. And she comforted me.

It's easy to lose perspective when you have little kids. One of the hardest things about this season in your life is that you don't see many results of your training. Even though you try to teach kindness, your kids still fight. Although you pray for patience, you lose yours. You sing "Jesus loves me" until you are blue in the face, yet you wonder if it's really sinking in.

This is a season of input and training, and you are not likely to see the results of this training for years. That's hard because we really need to see tangible fruit of our labor. We live in an instant society. We expect instant results in so many other areas of our lives and then we don't experience it in raising our kids. We need to recognize that looking for immediate results is an unrealistic expectation.

We have to remember that God is patient. He is not in a hurry. He is not surprised by our mistakes. He knows and loves each one of our children even more than we do. And he has chosen the exact children in the exact birth order with the exact personalities for our family. He has given us our kids not merely so that we can raise them but also in order that they might be used by him to grow us up into the men and women he has created us to be. He will use our children in our lives. He is at work in our family even if we can't see it right now, even when we feel like a bad parent, even when we fear we have messed up our child forever!

We have to remember that there is no mess that God cannot redeem. He is not condemning us. Instead he is delighting in us! He is patiently working through us and in us. And as he does he will gently lead us.

SUSAN

> *He tends his flock like a shepherd:*
> *He gathers the lambs in his arms*
> *and carries them close to his heart;*
> *he gently leads those that have young.*

ISAIAH 40:11

Finding the Confidence to Pray

Perhaps you picked up this book because you know you should be praying for your child. Or perhaps a friend gave it to you because he or she wanted to encourage you.

But let's be honest. You *may* be thinking, *I can't do this. After all, there is so much in my own life that isn't right. I don't even know if I really believe anyone will hear my prayer. I don't really know if I have faith myself, so how can I pray for my child?*

You are not alone. At some point in life most people have had similar thoughts. We wonder if God really is there. We wonder if he does care. We even question if it is possible to have a relationship with him when our own lives fall so far short of how we think he expects us to live.

Perhaps we *hope* it is all true, and we *hope* we have a relationship with him. Yet still, there is a glimmer of doubt.

I (Susan) grew up in a Christian home. I can't remember a time when I didn't believe in God or in his Son, Jesus. I tried to read my Bible, but it wasn't especially meaningful. I assumed that being a Christian meant being good. And that when I died if I'd been just a little bit more good than bad, I'd get to go to heaven. When I was a college student I met some intriguing graduate students. One of them asked me, "Susan, are you a Christian?"

"Well," I responded, thinking this was a very odd question coming from a cute guy, "I think I am. I hope I am."

My wise friend replied, "Susan, God doesn't want you to *think* you are or to *hope* that you are. He wants you to *know* that you are a believer."

He went on to tell me that God loved me and had a specific plan for my life. But I, like everyone else, was sinful (selfish) and separated from God. No one could be good enough for God. My good works would never get me "there." Yet God didn't leave me in this state. He sent his Son, Jesus, to die for my sins in order that I might be able to approach and to know God personally. Then my friend shared a promise from the Bible with me. The verse is meant to be a symbol of a picture of Christ standing at the door of our heart. It says, "Here I am! I stand at the door and knock. If anyone hears my voice and opens the door, I will come in" (Rev. 3:20).

My friend asked me, "Susan, have you ever asked Christ to come into your life, to be your personal Savior?"

I realized that I had not. Instead, because of my background, I had been living on an inherited faith, the faith of my parents. I needed a personal faith.

My friend asked me if I would like to pray and ask Christ to come into my life. Although there was much I didn't understand and this seemed a bit odd, I knew that it was something I needed and wanted to do. And so I did. My friend prayed out loud and I followed silently using his words and asked Christ to come into my life.

For me it wasn't an emotional experience. It was moving from an inherited faith to a personal faith. For others this decision is emotional. We are all different and God meets each of us in our own uniqueness.

My friend Barbara grew up in a scientific, agnostic home. Matters of faith were rarely discussed. She went into marriage and parenting with no religious background or any real interest in God. Yet as she and her husband encountered the challenges of the corporate world, marriage, and parenting, they realized they needed something. They felt there had to be something more to life, a deeper purpose. They wanted help as they raised their kids and began to look for God.

In time they too came to the place where each of them asked Christ to come into their lives and to come into the heart of their family.

It doesn't matter what our background is or what we've done or not done. God longs for each of us to come to him right where we are. He wants us to have the certainty of knowing him personally, not simply having a vague hope that he exists.

Friend, if you aren't sure that you've ever asked Christ into your heart and you would like to, I'm going to share a prayer similar to the one that my friend prayed with me. I would encourage you to pray this prayer for yourself and ask him to come into your heart.

Dear Jesus, I need you. I open the door of my heart and ask you to come in. Thank you for forgiving all my sins. Thank you for promising that you will never leave me. Thank you for the assurance that one day I'll be in heaven with you, not because I'm good but because I'm forgiven.

When you ask Christ to come into your heart several things happen.

1. He comes in!

You may or may not have experienced strong feelings. If you have, that's wonderful. But if you haven't, don't worry. Feelings or lack of feelings don't determine Christ's coming into our life. He comes in response to being asked. Our relationship with him is not based on our feelings. (What a relief!) It is based on faith in the fact that he will do what he has promised.

> *Here I am! I stand at the door and knock. If anyone hears my voice and opens the door, I will come in and eat with him, and he with me.*
>
> REVELATION 3:20

> *A faith and knowledge resting on the hope of eternal life, which God, who does not lie, promised before the beginning of time.*
>
> TITUS 1:2

2. He promises that he will never leave you.

Even when you forget him or mess up, he will never leave you.

> *God has said, "Never will I leave you; never will I forsake you."*
>
> HEBREWS 13:5

> *Where can I go from your Spirit?*
> *Where can I flee from your presence?*
> *If I go up to the heavens, you are there;*

114

if I make my bed in the depths, you are there.
If I rise on the wings of the dawn,
    if I settle on the far side of the sea,
even there your hand will guide me,
    your right hand will hold me fast.

PSALM 139:7–10

3. All your sins are forgiven.

When you ask him to forgive your sins, he does. Yes, even that one you can barely admit. He has forgiven that one too. And he stands ready to forgive your future sins when you mess up. All you need to do is to confess and ask for his forgiveness.

> *If we confess our sins, he is faithful and just and will forgive us our sins and purify us from all unrighteousness.*
> 1 JOHN 1:9

> *As far as the east is from the west,*
>   *so far has he removed our transgressions from us.*
> PSALM 103:12

4. You can know that one day you will be in heaven with him.

Going to heaven isn't dependent on being good. You could never be good enough. No one can. It is dependent on Christ taking your sins on his shoulders to the cross.

> *And this is the testimony: God has given us eternal life, and this life is in his Son. He who has the Son has life; he who does not have the Son of God does not have life.*
> 1 JOHN 5:11–12

115

5. He has given you his Holy Spirit to give you the power to live the life he has planned for you to live.

It isn't up to you to "grit your teeth and try harder." Christ has given you the full power of the Holy Spirit to enable you to become the person he has created you to be. You can't do it alone; that is not his intention. His intention is that you become more and more dependent upon him. When you rely on his Holy Spirit you will experience his supernatural power and freedom.

> *But the Counselor, the Holy Spirit, whom the Father will send in my name, will teach you all things and will remind you of everything I have said to you.*
>
> JOHN 14:26

> *But when he, the Spirit of truth, comes, he will guide you into all truth. He will not speak on his own; he will speak only what he hears, and he will tell you what is yet to come.*
>
> JOHN 16:13

6. You have a new family of brothers and sisters in Christ who will help you grow in him.

Just as our children go through different physical growth stages, you will go through different stages in your spiritual growth. It's so important to have friends to whom you can go with your spiritual questions. There is no question, or doubt, or feeling that is silly or insignificant. It helps to have others who have "been there" to guide the way. I encourage you to seek out a church whose teachings are based on the authority of Scripture and to find a small group in which to be involved for encouragement.

That which was from the beginning, which we have heard, which we have seen with our eyes, which we have looked at and our hands have touched—this we proclaim concerning the Word of life. The life appeared; we have seen it and testify to it, and we proclaim to you the eternal life, which was with the Father and has appeared to us. We proclaim to you what we have seen and heard, so that you also may have fellowship with us. And our fellowship is with the Father and with his Son, Jesus Christ. We write this to make our joy complete.

1 JOHN 1:1–4

Therefore encourage one another and build each other up, just as in fact you are doing.

1 THESSALONIANS 5:11

7. You have a certainty of Christ in your life, and for your children this will be a refuge.

Young children are especially open to spiritual truths. You may want to use this same section to explain to your child that he too can ask Christ into his heart. If he seems to understand, you may want to pray with him and let him ask Jesus to come into his own heart. It can be very special to record a description of this important step. When our children receive Christ, they become our brothers and sisters in him, and we begin to grow together. What joy!

People were also bringing babies to Jesus to have him touch them. When the disciples saw this, they rebuked them. But Jesus called the children to him and said, "Let the little children come to me,

117

and do not hinder them, for the kingdom of God belongs to such as these. I tell you the truth, anyone who will not receive the kingdom of God like a little child will never enter it."

LUKE 18:15–17

For whoever does the will of my Father in heaven is my brother and sister and mother.

MATTHEW 12:50

No longer do you have to think or hope or wonder if you are a believer. Now you are a "know so" believer. You know so because Jesus promised he would come into your heart if you ask him to. And he keeps his promises.

The Bible says, "In him and through faith in him we may approach God with freedom and confidence" (Eph. 3:12). And so, dear friend, you and I can approach God with every single concern that we have about our child. Nothing is too silly. Nothing will shock him. Nothing is too difficult for him to handle. He longs for us to come to him and to share our heart with him just as you and I long for our child to come and confide in us. He loves us even more than we love our child, so just imagine how much it thrills him when we come to him.

I pray that as you continue to use this book again and again to pray for your young child, your heart will be touched in a deep way with a fresh glimpse of how much your heavenly Father loves you.

SUSAN

The Daily Blessing

Don't we all love to give our children good gifts? The practice of saying a daily biblical blessing is an invaluable gift—one that builds up the child, protects him, encourages him, and gives him a sense of security in a frightening world. Simply choose words from Scripture, personalize them by saying your child's name, and repeat the words to the child as a daily prayer. Each time you repeat the blessing, you remind yourself and your child that he is safely entrusted to his Father.

I began saying daily blessings at bedtime when my three children were very young. For many years, I used the same blessing for each of them. I would place my hand on each child's head as a sign of covering and protection and say, using the child's name at the beginning, "Child, may the Lord bless you and keep you. May the Lord make his face shine

upon you and be gracious to you. May the Lord lift up his
countenance upon you and give you his peace. In the name
of the Father and of the Son and of the Holy Spirit, Amen."
This blessing is taken from Numbers 6:24–26.

I have since chosen other blessings for two of the children
using different portions of Scripture so that each child's blessing would be unique. The possibilities are as many and varied
as is Scripture. The most important ingredients are love and
consistency. Like all things upon which God smiles, these
daily blessings have brought our family countless rewards.

Blessing our children is one simple way in which we can
imitate Jesus. Remember when the children crowded around
him and the disciples tried to shoo them away because he
had more important things to do? Jesus scolded the disciples
and "took the children in his arms, put his hands on them
and blessed them" (Mark 10:16).

Over the years I've gone through long periods when I have
neglected these daily blessings. Now as I look back, I wonder
what all those "more important" things were for which I
gave up the few precious moments each day for blessing my
children. The good news is that it's never too late to begin
afresh. Whether your child is three or thirty, today is a fine
day to begin giving the gift of a daily blessing.

Here are some suggestions—personalize them with your
child's name:

1. "May the God of hope fill you with all joy and peace as
   you trust in him, so that you may overflow with hope
   by the power of the Holy Spirit" (Rom. 15:13).
2. "May God himself, the God of peace, sanctify you
   through and through. May your whole spirit, soul and
   body be kept blameless at the coming of our Lord Jesus
   Christ. The one who calls you is faithful and he will do

it. The grace of our Lord Jesus Christ be with you" (1 Thess. 5:23–24, 28).

3. "And the God of love and peace will be with you. May the grace of the Lord Jesus Christ, and the love of God, and the fellowship of the Holy Spirit be with you" (2 Cor. 13:11, 14).

4. "The LORD watches over you—the LORD is your shade at your right hand; the sun will not harm you by day, nor the moon by night. The LORD will keep you from all harm—he will watch over your life; the LORD will watch over your coming and going both now and forevermore" (Ps. 121:5–8).

5. "May our Lord Jesus Christ himself and God our Father, who loved us and by his grace gave us eternal encouragement and good hope, encourage your hearts and strengthen you in every good deed and word. May the Lord direct your hearts into God's love and Christ's perseverance. Now may the Lord of peace himself give you peace at all times and in every way" (2 Thess. 2:16–17; 3:5, 16).

6. May you be filled with the fruit of the Spirit—"love, joy, peace, patience, kindness, goodness, faithfulness, gentleness and self-control" (Gal. 5:22–23).

ELIZABETH FITCH

Elizabeth and her husband Wray live in McLean, Virginia. They have a seventeen-year-old daughter and twin twenty-one-year-old sons. Elizabeth offers personal growth coaching, seminars, and retreats.

Resources
for Mothering

Books for Parents

And Then I Had Kids: Encouragement for Mothers of Young Children
Susan Alexander Yates (Grand Rapids: Baker, 2002).

This is the book from which the book you are holding evolved. It is designed to be your basic guide on parenting young children. In it I discuss the common challenges we face as we raise our kids. Topics include: maintaining a positive self-image, seeing life in seasons, establishing priorities that work, becoming a best friend in marriage, solving the discipline dilemma, creating a loving atmosphere in the home, finding good role models for our families, shaping a creative Christian home, and looking ahead to the teen years and beyond.

Questions at the end of each chapter make this book easy to use in a small group setting. It is a helpful book for an older mom to use in reaching out to some young mothers in her neighborhood or church.

Audience: For all mothers of children 8 and under
For further information see: Yatesbooks.com

Character Matters! Raising Kids with Values That Last
John and Susan Yates (Grand Rapids: Baker, 2002).

In this book we highlight eight character traits we want our kids to develop: integrity, a teachable spirit, self-discipline, compassion, a servant's heart, courage, faith, and joy. Character is something that is developed in the everyday issues of life. We identify goals and suggest practical ways of achieving these goals. In the process we, the parents, will discover that we too need to grow in these same traits.

This book has a complete leader's guide in the appendix as well as questions at the end of each chapter. It is easy to use in an adult Sunday school class or in a neighborhood small group. It's excellent to use in an outreach ministry. We encourage you to include single parents in your small group.

Audience: Anyone with kids ages 5–18
For further information see: Yatesbooks.com

Building a Home Full of Grace
John and Susan Yates and Family (Grand Rapids: Baker, 2003).

This is your basic book on building a Christian home. We look at three essential commitments that are necessary to shape a family. And we look at different seasons in a family's life, from the arrival of that first child, to the teen years, to preparing your child for independence. Along the way we discuss building character, establishing discipline, creating a loving atmosphere, and praying for your family. Our kids have written some of the chapters in this book.

Audience: Anyone desiring to build a Christian family; this book makes a nice wedding gift

For further information see: Yatesbooks.com

31 Days of Praise
Ruth Myers (Sisters, OR: Multnomah, 1994).

This is one of our favorite devotional books. It has served as a template for the book you are now reading. In Myers's book, we learn how to take our problems to God and then focus on who he is and how much he loves to hear what's on our hearts. We receive assurance that he is able to handle all our concerns.

Audience: A great book for anyone of any age

Different Children, Different Needs
Charlie Boyd (Sisters, OR: Multnomah, 1994).

This book will teach you how to tailor your own unique parenting style to meet the different personalities of your children. It comes with a study guide and is helpful to use in a small group or as a couple.

Audience: Parents with kids of any age

Raising Sons and Loving It
Gary and Carrie Oliver (Grand Rapids: Zondervan, 2000).

Boys can be different! The Olivers give fun and sage advice for parenting and enjoying your sons.

Audience: Parents of boys

Watchmen on the Walls: Praying Character into Your Child
Anne Arkins and Gary Harrell (Sisters, OR: Multnomah, 1998).

Weekly selections of prayers for your child based on developing the following character traits: kindness, humility, teachability, forgiveness, obedience, discernment, purity, responsibility, courage, servanthood, contentment, and endurance.

Audience: Parents of children of all ages

Praying the Scriptures for Your Children
Jodie Berndt (Grand Rapids: Zondervan, 2001).

This is an instructional guide for praying for your children. It includes a rich treasure of true stories, practical prayers, and relevant Scriptures for our children.

Audience: Parents of children of all ages

Faith Like a Child: Discover the Simple Joy of Loving God
Johnny Parker (Grand Rapids: Revell, 2003).

Johnny Parker shares simple stories from his parenting that turn the mundane into the sublime. He reminds us in delightful ways that to enter the kindom of God we must become like children.

Audience: Anyone will find encouragement in this book!

Books for Sharing with Your Children

I Believe in Jesus: Leading Your Child to Christ
John MacArthur (Nashville: Tommy Nelson, 1999).

This wonderfully illustrated children's book helps parents explain the gospel story to their child. It is designed to be read aloud with your child.

Audience: Children ages 4–8

Read-Aloud Bible Stories
Ella Lindvall (Chicago: Moody, 1982).

We recommend any of the books by Ella Lindvall. Simple and wonderfully illustrated by Kent Puckett, they are great for children ages 2–5.

The Young Learner's Storybook
Dr. Mary Manz Simon (Cincinnati: Standard Publishing, 2002).

This Bible story book has fifty-two stories and over one hundred activities for you to do with your child. It is geared toward children ages 3–7. Dr. Simon is the author of many children's books (for all ages). We recommend all of her resources; they are excellent.

Additional Resources

If you are interested in getting connected with other mothers of young children, there is probably an organized group near you! We suggest that you visit the following websites for information on local groups and/or mothering resources:

- www.MOPS.org—Mothers of Preschoolers is an international organization designed specifically to meet the needs of mothers of young children. Local groups generally meet monthly, providing child care, fellowship, creative activities, and instruction in mothering.
- www.momsintouch.org—Moms in Touch is a group that meets to pray for their children and their schools.
- www.hearts-at-home.org—Another organization, also with local groups, which exists to encourage moms!
- www.familylife.com—Helpful resources for every stage of parenting.

Susan Alexander Yates is the author of ten books including the best selling, *And Then I Had Kids: Encouragement For Mothers Of Young Children*. She and her husband John have five grown children. They speak on marriage and parenting nationally and internationally. Susan is also a regular contributor to *Today's Christian Woman* magazine. The Yates live in Falls Church, Virginia.

Allison Yates Gaskins is author of *Tightening the Knot*, *Thanks, Mom, for Everything*, and *Thanks, Dad, for Everything*. Allison is expecting her fourth child and lives with her family in Ligonier, Pennsylvania. She received a B.A. at the University of Virginia. She married Will Gaskins in 1994 and taught French and U.S. History before having children. Allison has been involved in ministry since 1994. Her hobbies include reading, running, and remodeling homes with her husband.

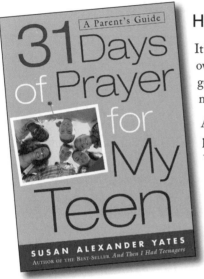
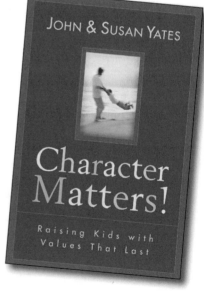